DAVID WENTZ

John Wesley's The New Birth

Set in Modern Language with Introduction and Suggestions for Group Use

DOING CHRISTIANITY

Pastor David Wentz

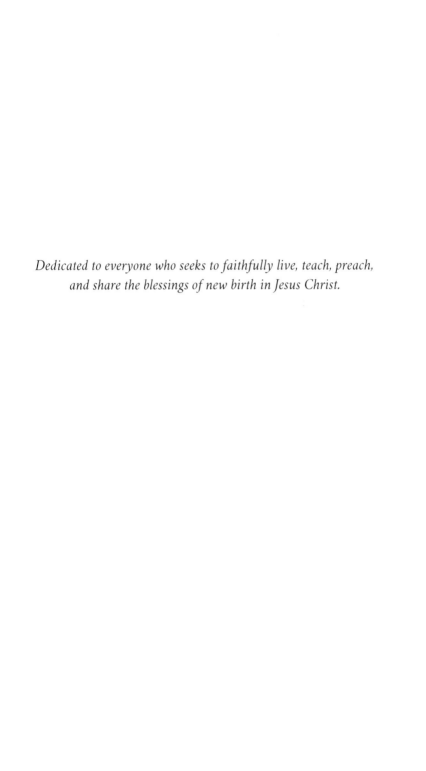

Dedicated to everyone who seeks to faithfully live, teach, preach, and share the blessings of new birth in Jesus Christ.

"You must be born again."

— Jesus

Contents

John Wesley was the son of an Anglican priest. He was baptized as an infant and raised in the church. He received Bachelor's and Master's degrees from Oxford University and taught Greek, philosophy, and New Testament there. He created a detailed systematic method for living a good moral religious life and practiced it faithfully — in fact, he and his followers were so strict about his holiness method that they were derisively called "method-ists." From 1735 to 1738 he served as a missionary in the American colony of Georgia. If anyone qualified for heaven based on religion and good works, it was John Wesley.

Then, on May 24, 1738, he experienced what Jesus meant. It wasn't a ritual. It wasn't self-discipline. It wasn't intellectual acceptance of a new theological idea. It wasn't an emotional high. It wasn't something he just had to take on faith. It was an experience. He wrote in his journal,

> I felt my heart strangely warmed. I felt I did trust in Christ, Christ alone for salvation; and an assurance was given me that He had taken away my sins, even mine, and saved me from the law of sin and death.[1]

John Wesley had experienced the new birth. And he began to preach about it.

Wesley's teachings and writings were clear, logical, and Biblical. His preaching was forceful and fiery. And of course, his follow-up and organizing skills were methodical. The combination sparked a revival that could not be contained in the established church. Its effects are still felt today. The numerous Methodist and Wesleyan denominations and the Salvation Army, as well as the holiness and Pentecostal movements, all trace their lineage back to John Wesley and his experience of the new birth.

In Wesley's day, Wesley's followers were often violently persecuted. Their fierce belief, faithful lives, and bold witness threatened the complacency of those who put their trust in rituals and reputation.

Almost three hundred years later, people who attend the churches that descended from Wesley's teaching are rarely called fanatics. In fact, it's often hard to tell them apart from their neighbors who don't go to church at all.

Some people still think they have a golden ticket to heaven because they were baptized. Most believe that as long as they score in the top 50% on a morality test they have it made. As far as the new birth is concerned, they either think they've already experienced it, or they think they don't need it. If that's you, John Wesley has a message for you.

Wesley's logic, clarity, and Biblical truth are as potent today as they ever were. Unfortunately, his eighteenth-century English is more and more difficult for modern readers to understand. Wesley was a revival preacher with the best of them, with people often being so struck by his words that they cried out and even fell to the ground. Today, the mental effort of interpreting his phrases can rob them of their power.

That's where this book helps. It updates Wesley's English to be clear to the modern reader while maintaining his distinctive writing and preaching style. My goal is not only to help you understand Wesley's points but to give a sense of what it was like to hear him preach. For scholars and the curious, Wesley's original is included as an appendix.

I believe Wesley would approve. He wrote,

> I design plain truth for plain people. . . I labor to
> avoid all words which are not easy to be understood,
> all which are not used in common life.[2]

John Wesley habitually preached at least twice a day, usually outdoors to anyone who would listen. As his movement grew, Wesley gathered his most important sermons into a book which he published for his lay preachers to read, learn, and then preach in their own words. *The New Birth* is one of them. While you can read it straight through, as Wesley's original listeners would have heard it, I've broken it up here into bite-size sections to make it easier to discuss and digest.

As you go through this study you're likely to come across some statements that strike you as unrealistic, if not downright radical. That was John Wesley. These were the things he taught. I can make the language easier for our minds to understand, but I can't make his statements any easier for our human nature to accept.

But isn't the same true of many things Jesus said? Wesley just took Jesus' words, clearly explained them, and carried them to their logical conclusion, without the exceptions and excuses we so often like to add. The result is a whole new way of living, made possible not by human willpower but by a new spiritual birth.

What would it look like if we were to rediscover this Wesleyan ideal? What would it look like if every local church in every denomination that traces its heritage back to Wesley were to become known as a place where people are actively trying to live the kind of new life Wesley describes?

Frankly, we might lose some members at first, because this is not an easy feel-good religion. But if people today are anything like they were when Wesley preached – and I believe they are, because human nature doesn't change – a lot of people would find this type of Christianity immensely attractive.

Wesley's method for finding spiritual truth

In the Preface to a collection of his sermons, Wesley explained his method for finding spiritual truth:[3]

> To candid, reasonable people I am not afraid to lay open what have been the inmost thoughts of my heart. I have thought, I am a creature of the day, passing through life, as an arrow through the air. I am a spirit come from God, and returning to God: just hovering over the great gulf; till a few moments from now, I am no more seen! I drop into an unchangeable eternity! I want to know one thing, the way to heaven: how to land safe on that happy shore.
>
> God himself has condescended to teach the way. For this very reason he came from heaven. He has written it down in a book! Oh give me that book! At any price, give me the book of God!
>
> I have it! Here is knowledge enough for me. Let me be a man of one book.
>
> Here I am then, far from the busy ways of people. I sit down alone. Only God is here. And in his presence I open and read this book. My purpose: to find the way to heaven.

Is there a doubt concerning the meaning of something I read?   Does anything appear unclear or confusing?

I lift up my heart to the Father of lights, praying: *Lord, doesn't your word say, If anyone lacks wisdom, let him ask of God?   You give generously and ungrudgingly.[4] You said if anyone is willing to do your will, they shall know.[5] I am willing! Let me know your will.*

Then I search after and consider parallel passages of scripture, comparing spiritual things with spiritual.[6]

I meditate on it,[7] with all the attention and earnestness of which my mind is capable.

If any doubt still remains, I consult those who are experienced in the things of God, and the writings of those who have gone before.

And what I learn in this way, that is what I teach.

Notes on the Paraphrase

Though one of the most widely read men of his time, here John Wesley says he wanted to be a man of one book. That book was the Bible. His sermons are liberally sprinkled with Scripture quotations and allusions. Wesley's Bible was the *King James Version* (KJV), translated in 1611. For many modern readers, that English can be even more difficult than Wesley's. So for the Bible references in this paraphrase, I chose either the *New Revised Standard Version* or the *New King James Version*. Both are clear, accurate translations that trace their literary lineage back to the *King James* Bible. The *New Revised Standard* is more widely used in Methodist churches, so that was my first choice. In some cases, where the *New King James* more closely reflected Wesley's wording, I used that translation, with the notation NKJV. I also tried to provide Scripture references for the many places where Wesley alluded to Scripture without specifically quoting it.

In Wesley's day the words "he," "him" and "his" were understood to refer to both men and women equally, unless context indicated otherwise. This is not the case today. However, the English language has not yet developed an easy alternative expression. In updating Wesley's words, rather than force awkward constructions I have chosen to alternate gender pronouns by section. As should be obvious, both "he" and "she" are intended to be representative of all people.

Finally, the methodical Wesley commonly used the technique of numbering his paragraphs. I have replaced the numbers with chapter titles and subheadings and divided his long block paragraphs into shorter ones to reflect modern usage.

Suggestions for Group Use

John Wesley wrote *The New Birth* as a sermon, and this version can certainly be read straight through in that way. However, as with all thought-provoking books, Wesley's words will have the greatest impact on our individual lives and on our churches when we discuss them with others.

That was part of Wesley's method. He organized his followers into small groups called classes which met weekly, usually in people's homes. Their main purpose was to discuss how they could be better Christians, based on the previous week's sermon, and to hold each other accountable for acting that way. As they met, they experienced a joyful fellowship. In the modern phrase, they were "doing life together."

This book is perfectly suited for that kind of small-group experience. It can be a home group, a coffee shop gathering, or an adult Sunday School class. To facilitate such use, I've broken the material into six parts. Each should take less than fifteen minutes to read. I've also included some suggested discussion questions at the end of each part, to get you started.

How to Lead a Small Group

Small group gatherings are easy. You can meet in the same place every time, or in different people's homes. You can have the same leader every time, or rotate leadership. (Being the leader isn't a big deal. The leader is just the person who reads the discussion questions out loud.) A good time frame is an hour to an hour and a half. The tried and true format goes something like this:

- People arrive, say hello, and perhaps munch on some light refreshments.
- Somebody says a prayer to get things started, asking God to guide the conversation and bless anyone who is missing.
- You catch up on anything left over from last week – especially including any good stories about how the study

helped someone during the week.

- You talk about the discussion questions. Answer the ones that interest you, or make up your own.
- You set the place, time, and assignments for the next meeting.
- You share prayer concerns and pray for them.
- You go out and live what you learned.

If anyone was absent, the leader or a designated person should call them within a day. Tell them you missed them, see if anything is wrong, and catch them up on what happened. Don't forget to tell them the details of the next meeting.

Suggested Schedule

Six weeks is a good, non-threatening length of time for most people to commit to a study like this. Here is a suggested six-week schedule.

Week 1: Introduction

Week 2: What's Wrong With the Old Birth?

Week 3: How to Be Born Again

Week 4: What Does the New Birth Do?

Week 5: Myths About the New Birth

Week 6: A Warning to the Spiritually Unborn

Discussion Questions

1. What is your church background?
   A denomination or tradition that traces back to John Wesley?
   Another Christian denomination or tradition?
   A Christian church but you're not sure of the roots?
   A variety of different churches?
   Not raised as a church-goer?

2. Do you believe there is value in knowing the historic roots of your faith tradition?
   Why or why not?

3. Would you describe yourself as a born-again Christian?
   If so, what does that mean to you?
   If not, why not?

4. What have you been taught about what it takes to get to heaven?

5. The introduction states that millions of people attend the churches that descended from Wesley's teaching, but it's often hard to tell them apart from their neighbors who don't go to church at all.
   Do you agree?
   If you agree, why do you think that is the case?
   Does it matter if it's hard to tell Christians from other people?

6. Does Wesley's method for finding spiritual truth seem reasonable for modern Christians?
   Why or why not?

7. What do you hope to gain from this study?

Notes

[1] *Journal of John Wesley*, entry for May 24, 1738

[2] "Preface to the Sermons," from *The Works of John Wesley,* Third American Edition

[3] Language updated.

[4] *If any of you is lacking in wisdom, ask God, who gives to all generously and ungrudgingly, and it will be given you.* (James 1:5)

[5] *Thus says the Lord, your Redeemer, the Holy One of Israel: I am the Lord your God, who teaches you for your own good, who leads you in the way you should go.* (Isaiah 48:17)

[6] *These things we also speak, not in words which man's wisdom teaches but which the Holy Spirit teaches, comparing spiritual things with spiritual.* (1 Corinthians 2:13 NKJV)

[7] *This book of the law shall not depart out of your mouth, you shall meditate on it day and night, so that you may be careful to act in accordance with all that is written in it. For then you shall make your way prosperous, and then you shall be successful."* (Joshua 1:8)

1

What's Wrong With the Old Birth?

If any doctrines in all of Christian belief can properly be called foundational, without doubt they are these two: the doctrine of justification, and the doctrine of the new birth. Justification relates to that great work God does for us, in forgiving our sins; the new birth relates to the great work God does in us, in renewing our fallen human nature.

In order of time, neither of these happens before the other: the moment we are justified by the grace of God through the redemption that is in Jesus, that same moment we are also born of the Spirit.[1] But in order of how we think about it, justification comes before the new birth. We first think of God's anger toward sin to be turned away, and then his Holy Spirit to work in our hearts.

Given the eternal consequences, how important it is for every human being to thoroughly understand these fundamental doctrines!

From a full conviction of this, many excellent scholars have written quite a lot about justification, explaining every point relating to it, and explaining the Scriptures that deal with it.

Many have also written about the new birth, and some of them with many words. But it seems to me that on this topic none of them have written as clearly as might have been desired, nor as deeply and accurately. Either they gave a dense, confusing account of it, or a slight and superficial one. Therefore a full, and at the same time a clear, account of the new birth, seems to be still lacking; one that can enable us to give a satisfactory answer to these three questions:

1. Why must we be born again? What need underlies this doctrine of the new birth?
2. How must we be born again? What is the nature of the new birth?
3. What is the purpose of being born again? To what end or goal is it necessary?

These questions, by the assistance of God, I shall briefly and plainly answer. Then I will add a few conclusions that naturally follow.

First, why must we be born again? What need underlies this doctrine?

God created humans in his image

The foundation of the doctrine of the new birth lies nearly as deep as the creation of the world. In the Scriptural account of creation we read, *Then God,* the three-one God, *said, "Let us make humankind in our image, according to our likeness"* . . . *So God created humankind in his image, in the image of God he created them; male and female he created them.*[2]

God did not create them merely in the image of God's nature, as a picture of his own immortality; spiritual beings endued with understanding, freedom of will, and various affections. He did not create them just in what we might call his political image, as governors over this lower world, with dominion over the fish of the sea, and over all the earth. God chiefly created them in his moral image, which, according to the apostle Paul, is true righteousness and holiness.[3] This is the image in which humankind was made.

God is love;[4] therefore, humans at creation were full of love. It was the sole principle of all their attitudes, thoughts, words, and actions.

God is full of justice, mercy, and truth; so were humans as they came from the hands of their Creator.

God is spotless purity; and so humans, in the beginning, were pure from every sinful blot. Otherwise, God could not have called them "very good," as he did all the other work of his hands.[5] They could not have been "very good" unless they were pure from sin and filled with righteousness and true holiness. For there is no middle ground: if we imagine an intelligent creature that does not love God, that is not righteous and holy, then it stands to reason that it cannot be good at all, much less "very good."

Our first ancestors rebelled and lost the image of God

But, although humans were made in the image of God, they were not made unchanging, as God is.[6] This would have been inconsistent with the state of trial in which God chose to place them. They were therefore created able to stand, and yet liable to fall.

God made the first humans aware of this and gave them a solemn warning against it. Nevertheless, they did not honor the warning, and they fell from their high position. They ate from the tree from which God commanded them not to eat.[7] By this willful act of disobedience to their Creator, this flat rebellion against their King, they openly declared that they would no longer have God to rule over them; that they would be governed by their own will and not the will of the one who created them; and that they would not seek their happiness in God but in the world, in the works of their own hands.

Now God had told them before, "in the day you eat of [that fruit] you shall die."[8] And the word of the Lord cannot be broken. Accordingly, in that day they did die. They died to God — the most dreadful of all deaths. They lost the life of God: their spiritual life was in being united with God, and they were separated from him. The body dies when it is separated from the soul; the soul dies when it is separated from God.

But this separation from God happened to Adam and Eve in the day, the hour, when they ate the forbidden fruit. And they gave immediate proof of this. They showed by their behavior that the love of God was extinguished in their souls and they were now alienated from the life of God.[9] Instead, they were now under the power of cowardly fear. They fled from the presence of the Lord. In fact, they retained so little knowledge of the one who fills heaven and earth[10] that they tried to hide from the Lord God among the trees of the garden.[11] That is how much they had lost both the knowledge and the love of God. And without them, the image of God could not exist. So they lost that at the same time, and became unholy as well as unhappy. Instead, they had sunk into pride and self-will, the very image of the devil; and into sensual appetites and desires, the image of the animals that perish.

Someone might say, "No, you have it wrong. That warning, 'in the day you eat of it you shall die,' only refers to temporal death. It just means the death of the body."

The answer is plain: to say that is flatly and blatantly to call God a liar. It is to claim that the God of truth positively affirmed a thing contrary to truth. Because it is evident that Adam and Eve did not die in a physical sense the same day they ate the fruit. Adam lived physically more than nine hundred years longer.[12] So this verse cannot possibly be understood to mean the death of the body, without impeaching the veracity of God. It must therefore be understood to mean spiritual death, the loss of the life and image of God.

Every human since Adam and Eve has been born lacking the image of God

And when Adam died everyone died,[13] all humankind, every one of Adam's descendants. The natural consequence of this is, that everyone descended from Adam comes into the world spiritually dead: dead to God, completely dead in sin, entirely empty of the life of God, and empty of the image of God, of all that righteousness and holiness in which Adam was created. Instead of this, every person born into the world now bears the image of the devil in pride and self-will, and the image of the animals, in sensual appetites and desires.

This, then, is the underlying reason why we need a new birth: our human nature is entirely corrupted. This is why, being born in sin, we must be born again. This is why everyone that is born of a woman must be born of the Spirit of God.[14]

Discussion Questions

1. "If any doctrines in all of Christian belief can properly be called foundational, without doubt they are these two: the doctrine of justification, and the doctrine of the new birth."

Are you surprised that Wesley picked these two doctrines as foundational?

Do you feel like you have a good understanding of these two doctrines?

Are there any other doctrines you would list as foundational to Christianity?

2. "There is no middle ground: if we imagine an intelligent creature that does not love God, that is not righteous and holy, then it stands to reason that it cannot be good at all, much less 'very good.'"

What makes a truly good person?

In light of this statement, can there be a truly good person who does not love God?

3. Wesley says God placed the first humans in a state of trial, able to stand, and yet liable to fall.

Why would God do that?

What would the relationship between God and humans be like if we were not free to choose disobedience?

4. "They ate from the tree from which God commanded them not to eat. By this willful act of disobedience to their Creator, this flat rebellion against their King, they openly declared that they would no longer have God to rule over them."

Think about a time you knowingly did something the Bible says not to do. Was it your intention to rebel against God and declare that you would no longer have him rule over you?

Even if that was not your intention, could it have had that effect?

5. "Everyone descended from Adam comes into the world spiritually dead: dead to God, completely dead in sin, entirely empty of the life of God, and empty of the image of God, of all that righteousness and holiness in which Adam was created. Instead of this, every person born into the world now bears the image of the devil in pride and self-will, and the image of the animals, in sensual appetites and desires."

What evidence can you see in the world that supports or refutes this statement?

From a spiritual perspective, what is the eternal result of this?

Notes

[1] *Jesus answered, "Very truly, I tell you, no one can enter the kingdom of God without being born of water and Spirit."* (John 3:5)

[2] *Then God said, "Let us make humankind in our image, according to our likeness; and let them have dominion over the fish of the sea, and over the birds of the air, and over the cattle, and over all the wild animals of the earth, and over every creeping thing that creeps upon the earth." So God created humankind in his image, in the image of God he created them; male and female he created them.* (Genesis 1:26-27)

[3] *And to clothe yourselves with the new self, created according to the likeness of God in true righteousness and holiness.* (Ephesians 4:24)

[4] *Whoever does not love does not know God, for God is love.* (1 John 4:8)

[5] *God saw everything that he had made, and indeed, it was very good. And there was evening and there was morning, the sixth day.* (Genesis 1:31)

[6] *For I the Lord do not change; therefore you, O children of Jacob, have not perished.* (Malachi 3:6)

[7] *He said, "Who told you that you were naked? Have you eaten from the tree of which I commanded you not to eat?" The man said, "The woman whom you gave to be with me, she gave me fruit from the tree, and I ate."* (Genesis 3:11–12)

[8] *And the Lord God commanded the man, "You may freely eat of every tree of the garden; but of the tree of the knowledge of good and evil you shall not eat, for in the day that you eat of it you shall die."* (Genesis 2:16–17)

[9] *They are darkened in their understanding, alienated from the life of God because of their ignorance and hardness of heart.* (Ephesians 4:18)

[10] *Who can hide in secret places so that I cannot see them? says the Lord. Do I not fill heaven and earth? says the Lord.* (Jeremiah 23:24)

[11] *They heard the sound of the Lord God walking in the garden at the time of the evening breeze, and the man and his wife hid themselves from the presence of the Lord God among the trees of the garden.*

(Genesis 3:8)

[12] *Thus all the days that Adam lived were nine hundred thirty years; and he died.* (Genesis 5:5)

[13] *Therefore, just as sin came into the world through one man, and death came through sin, and so death spread to all because all have sinned* (Romans 5:12)

For as all die in Adam, so all will be made alive in Christ. (1 Corinthians 15:22)

[14] *Jesus answered, "Very truly, I tell you, no one can enter the kingdom of God without being born of water and Spirit. What is born of the flesh is flesh, and what is born of the Spirit is spirit."* (John 3:5–6)

2

How to Be Born Again

But how is a person to be born again? What is the nature of the new birth? This is the second question. And it is the most important question that can be imagined. So we should not be content, in such a crucial matter, with just a brief inquiry. We must examine it with all possible care, and ponder it in our hearts, until we fully understand this important point, and clearly see how we are to be born again.

We can't explain it intellectually

Not that we are to expect any detailed philosophical account of the manner in which this is done. Our Lord Jesus sufficiently guards us against any such expectation by the words immediately following our opening verse. He reminds Nicodemus of a fact as indisputable as any in the whole realm of nature, and yet one which the wisest person under the sun is not able fully to explain. *The wind blows where it chooses* —not by your power

11

or wisdom; *and you hear the sound of it* — so you are absolutely assured, beyond all doubt, that it does blow; *but you do not know where it comes from or where it goes* — the precise way in which it begins and ends, rises and falls, no one can tell. *So it is with everyone who is born of the Spirit.*[1] You can be as absolutely sure of the new birth as you are that the wind is blowing; but exactly how it happens, how the Holy Spirit works this in the soul, neither you nor the wisest person is able to explain.

The meaning of "born again"

However, it's enough for every rational and Christian purpose that, without descending into arcane theological speculations, we can give a plain scriptural account of the nature of the new birth. This will satisfy every reasonable person whose main concern is the salvation of their soul.

The expression, "being born again," was not first used by our Lord in his conversation with Nicodemus. It was well known before that time, and was in common use among the Jews when our Savior appeared among them. When a heathen man became convinced that the Jewish religion was of God, and desired to join it, the custom was to baptize him first, before he was allowed to be circumcised. And when he was baptized, he was said to be born again. By this, they meant that this person used to be a child of the devil, but now he was adopted into the family of God and counted as one of God's children.

So Jesus used this expression in talking with Nicodemus, who, being a teacher of Israel, should have understood it well.[2] Only Jesus used it in a stronger sense than Nicodemus was used to.

That might be why he asked, "How can these things be?"[3]

They cannot be, literally — people cannot enter a second time into their mother's womb and be born a second time, physically.[4] But they can be, spiritually. A person may be born from above,[5] born of God,[6] born of the Spirit,[7] in a manner that in many ways closely parallels physical birth.

Spiritual birth parallels natural birth

Before a child is born into the world she has eyes, but does not really see; she has ears, but does not clearly hear. She has a very imperfect use of any other sense. She has no knowledge of any of the things of the world, and no natural understanding. She is alive, but not yet experiencing life as we usually think of it; that is why we count age from the day of birth. Because as soon as she is born, she begins to see the light, and the various objects around her. Her ears begin to clearly hear the sounds that come to them. At the same time, all the other organs of sense begin to work. She begins to breathe. She lives in a manner totally different from when she was in the womb.

The parallel is exact in all these examples! While a man is in a mere natural state, before he is born of God, he has spiritual eyes but cannot see;[8] a thick, impenetrable veil lies over them.[9] He has spiritual ears, but cannot hear; he is utterly deaf to what is most important for him to hear. His other spiritual senses are all locked up; he is in the same condition as if he did not even have them. So he has no knowledge of God, no interaction with him; he is not at all acquainted with him. He has no true knowledge of the things of God, either spiritual or eternal.[10]

As a man he is living, but as a Christian he is dead.

But as soon as a person is born of God, there is a total change in all these things. The eyes of her heart are opened, in the words of the great apostle.[11] God, who commanded light to shine out of darkness, now shines that light on her heart, and she sees the glory of God, her glorious love, in the face of Jesus Christ.[12] Her spiritual ears are opened, and she can now hear the inward voice of God saying, "Take heart, your sins are forgiven;[13] from now on do not sin again."[14] This is the meaning of what God speaks in her heart, though perhaps not in just those words.

She is now ready to hear whatever God who teaches knowledge to humankind[15] decides, from time to time, to reveal to her. In the words of the Church, she feels in her heart the mighty working of the Spirit of God. Worldly people in their ignorance choose to think this refers to some kind of crass or manipulated emotionalism. Instead, as we have explained time and again, what we mean is this: she senses, through an inward awareness, the good changes the Spirit of God is working in her heart. She feels, she is conscious of, the peace of God which surpasses all understanding.[16] She often feels a joy in God that is indescribable and glorious.[17] She feels the love of God that has been poured into her heart through the Holy Spirit that has been given to her.[18] All her spiritual senses go into action to discern spiritual good and evil.[19] By these things she daily increases in the knowledge of God, of Jesus Christ whom God sent, and of all the things that pertain to God's inward kingdom.

And now the person may be properly said to live! God brought him back to life by God's Spirit, and he is alive to God through Jesus Christ. He lives a life the world knows nothing about, a life hidden with Christ in God.[20] It's as if God

14

is continually breathing on his soul, and his soul is breathing back to God. Grace is coming down into his heart, and prayer and praise are rising to heaven. This interaction between God and human, this fellowship with the Father and the Son,[21] is a kind of spiritual respiration that sustains the life of God in the soul; and the child of God grows up spiritually until he reaches the measure of the full stature of Christ.[22]

The new birth changes things

From all this we can clearly see what the new birth is. It is that great change God works in the soul when he brings it into life, when he raises it from the death of sin to the life of righteousness. It is the change worked in the whole soul by the almighty Spirit of God when the soul is made new in Christ Jesus, when it is renewed according to the likeness of God in true righteousness and holiness.[23] The love of the world is changed into the love of God, pride into humility, passion into meekness. Hatred, envy, and malice, are changed into a sincere, tender, no-strings attached love for all humankind.

In a word, the new birth is that change by which the earthly, sensual, devilish mind is turned into the mind which was in Christ Jesus.[24] This is the nature of the new birth. This is how it is with everyone who is born of the Spirit.[25]

Discussion Questions

1. Why does Wesley say that the most important question that can be imagined is the question of how to be born again?

2. Have you ever heard someone use an expression like, "I felt like I was reborn" or, "I felt like I was given a whole new life," in a non-religious sense?

What did they mean by it?

How does that help you understand what Jesus was talking about in his conversation with Nicodemus?

3. If you consider yourself born-again, how well does Wesley's comparison between physical and spiritual birth describe your own experience?

What misunderstandings might result from carrying this comparison too far?

4. If the Bible and spiritual things seem to you vague, confusing, and superstitious, could it be that you have not yet been born again in the sense Wesley is describing? *Those who are unspiritual*

16

do not receive the gifts of God's Spirit, for they are foolishness to them, and they are unable to understand them because they are spiritually discerned. (1 Corinthians 2:14)

5. "She feels in her heart the mighty working of the Spirit of God. Worldly people in their ignorance choose to think this refers to some kind of crass or manipulated emotionalism."

How do you tell the difference between spiritual feelings and emotions?

Does this verse help? *Indeed, the word of God is living and active, sharper than any two-edged sword, piercing until it divides soul from spirit, joints from marrow; it is able to judge the thoughts and intentions of the heart.* (Hebrews 4:12)

What kind of ignorance is Wesley attributing to worldly people?

6. The last two paragraphs describe an experience and a change.

How well can you relate to these descriptions in your own life?

Are these changes the automatic result of being born again?

If not, what does the Christian need to do to continue to experience and grow in them?

Notes

[1] *The wind blows where it chooses, and you hear the sound of it, but you do not know where it comes from or where it goes. So it is with everyone who is born of the Spirit.* (John 3:8)

[2] *Jesus answered him, "Are you a teacher of Israel, and yet you do not understand these things?"* (John 3:10)

[3] *Nicodemus said to him, "How can these things be?"* (John 3:9)

[4] *Nicodemus said to him, "How can anyone be born after having grown old? Can one enter a second time into the mother's womb and be born?"* (John 3:4)

[5] *Born from above* is an alternate reading for John 3:7. The Greek word is *anothen.* It can refer to place, "from above;" or to time, "from the beginning," often in the sense of "start over again."

[6] *Everyone who believes that Jesus is the Christ has been born of God, and everyone who loves the parent loves the child.* (1 John 5:1)

[7] *Jesus answered, "Very truly, I tell you, no one can enter the kingdom of God without being born of water and Spirit."* (John 3:5)

[8] *Hear this, O foolish and senseless people, who have eyes, but do not see, who have ears, but do not hear.* (Jeremiah 5:21)

[9] *But their minds were hardened. Indeed, to this very day, when they hear the reading of the old covenant, that same veil is still there, since*

only in Christ is it set aside. (2 Corinthians 3:14)

[10] *Those who are unspiritual do not receive the gifts of God's Spirit, for they are foolishness to them, and they are unable to understand them because they are spiritually discerned.* (1 Corinthians 2:14)

[11] *I pray that the God of our Lord Jesus Christ, the Father of glory, may give you a spirit of wisdom and revelation as you come to know him, so that, with the eyes of your heart enlightened, you may know what is the hope to which he has called you, what are the riches of his glorious inheritance among the saints, and what is the immeasurable greatness of his power for us who believe, according to the working of his great power.* (Ephesians 1:17–19)

[12] *For it is the God who said, "Let light shine out of darkness," who has shone in our hearts to give the light of the knowledge of the glory of God in the face of Jesus Christ.* (2 Corinthians 4:6)

[13] *And just then some people were carrying a paralyzed man lying on a bed. When Jesus saw their faith, he said to the paralytic, "Take heart, son; your sins are forgiven."* (Matthew 9:2)

[14] *She said, "No one, sir." And Jesus said, "Neither do I condemn you. Go your way, and from now on do not sin again."* (John 8:11)

[15] *He who disciplines the nations, he who teaches knowledge to humankind, does he not chastise?* (Psalm 94:10)

[16] *And the peace of God, which surpasses all understanding, will guard your hearts and your minds in Christ Jesus.* (Philippians 4:7)

[17] *Although you have not seen him, you love him; and even though you do not see him now, you believe in him and rejoice with an indescribable and glorious joy.* (1 Peter 1:8)

[18] *And hope does not disappoint us, because God's love has been poured into our hearts through the Holy Spirit that has been given to us.* (Romans 5:5)

[19] *But solid food is for the mature, for those whose faculties have been trained by practice to distinguish good from evil.* (Hebrews 5:14)

[20] *for you have died, and your life is hidden with Christ in God.* (Colossians 3:3)

[21] *We declare to you what we have seen and heard so that you also may have fellowship with us; and truly our fellowship is with the Father and with his Son Jesus Christ.* (1 John 1:3)

[22] *Until all of us come to the unity of the faith and of the knowledge of the Son of God, to maturity, to the measure of the full stature of Christ.* (Ephesians 4:13)

[23] *And to clothe yourselves with the new self, created according to the likeness of God in true righteousness and holiness.* (Ephesians 4:24)

[24] *Let the same mind be in you that was in Christ Jesus,* (Philippians 2:5)

[25] *The wind blows where it chooses, and you hear the sound of it, but*

you do not know where it comes from or where it goes. So it is with everyone who is born of the Spirit. (John 3:8)

3

What Does the New Birth Do?

Once one thinks about these things it is not hard to see the need for the new birth, and to answer the third question: What is the purpose, to what end, is it necessary that we should be born again?

Holiness

It is very easy to see that the new birth is needed, first, for holiness.

For what is holiness, according to the word of God? Not a bare external religion, a round of outward duties, no matter how many we do or how well we do them. No! Gospel holiness is no less than the image of God stamped upon the heart. It is nothing else than having the whole mind which was in Christ Jesus.[1] It is all the heavenly feelings and attitudes mixed together in one.

It implies such a continual, thankful love to God, who did not withhold from us his Son, his only son, that it becomes natural, and in a way necessary, for us to love every other person. It fills us with compassion, kindness, humility, meekness, and patience.[2] This love of God teaches us to be blameless in all our interactions.[3] It enables us to present our souls and bodies, all we are and all we have, all our thoughts, words, and actions, as a continual sacrifice to God, acceptable through Christ Jesus.[4]

Now, this holiness can have no existence until we are renewed in our minds.[5] It cannot begin in the soul until that change has been worked; until, by the power of the Highest overshadowing us, we are brought from darkness to light, from the power of Satan to God[6]. In other words, until we are born again. So the new birth is absolutely necessary for holiness.

Salvation

But the Bible says without holiness no one will see the Lord,[7] no one will see the face of God in glory. That means the new birth is absolutely necessary for eternal salvation.

People may indeed persuade themselves (so desperately wicked and so deceitful is the human heart!)[8] that they can live in their sins until they come to the last gasp, and yet still live after death with God. And thousands do really believe they have found an easy road that doesn't lead to destruction.[9]

"What danger," they say, "can a woman be in who is good and never hurts anyone? What fear is there that an honest, moral man should miss heaven? Especially if, over and above all this, they go to church every Sunday and take Communion?" One of these will ask with all assurance, "What! Shall I not do as well as my neighbors?"

Yes, as well as your unholy neighbors; as well as your neighbors that die in their sins! For you will all drop into the pit together, into the lowest hell! You will all lie together in the lake of fire; "the lake of fire burning with brimstone."[10] Then, finally, you will see (but God grant you may see it before!) that holiness is necessary to reach glory. And that means the new birth is necessary, since no one can be holy unless they are born again.

Happiness

For the same reason, unless a person is born again, they cannot be happy even in this world. For it is not possible, in the nature of things, that a person should be happy who is not holy. Even an ancient pagan poet knew it, writing, "No wicked man is happy."[11]

The reason is plain: All unholy attitudes are uneasy attitudes. Not only malice, hatred, envy, jealousy, and revenge create hell in the heart; but even the softer passions, if not properly controlled, give a thousand times more pain than pleasure. Even hope, when deferred, (and how often must this be the case!) makes the heart sick.[12] Every desire that is not according to the will of God is liable to pierce us through with many sorrows.[13] And all those general sources of sin — pride, self-will, and idolatry — are, to the same degree that they prevail, general sources of misery.

Therefore, as long as these reign in any soul, happiness has no place there. But they must reign until the direction of our nature is changed; that is, until we are born again. Consequently, the new birth is absolutely necessary for happiness in this world, as well as in the world to come.

Discussion Questions

1. What do you think of when you hear the word "holiness?"

2. Is it possible to live a holy life through self-discipline and will-power?
　Why or why not?

3. In the section titled "Salvation," Wesley says good, honest, moral church-going people who never hurt anyone "will all drop into the pit together, into the lowest hell!"
　What was your first reaction on reading this?
　Is he saying all good church people will go to hell?
　If not, what is he saying?
　How would you support or refute this from the Bible?

4. "It is not possible, in the nature of things, that a person should be happy who is not holy."

When most people are asked to describe Christians, do you think the first word they think of is "happy?"

Why or why not?

In your own experience of church people, do most of them seem happier than people in general?

Why do you think that might be?

5. Do you find Wesley's reasoning in this chapter persuasive? If not, where is the flaw in his logic?

Notes

[1] *Let the same mind be in you that was in Christ Jesus.* (Philippians 2:5)

[2] *As God's chosen ones, holy and beloved, clothe yourselves with compassion, kindness, humility, meekness, and patience.* (Colossians 3:12)

[3] *So that you may be blameless and innocent, children of God without blemish in the midst of a crooked and perverse generation, in which you shine like stars in the world.* (Philippians 2:15)

[4] *I appeal to you therefore, brothers and sisters, by the mercies of God, to present your bodies as a living sacrifice, holy and acceptable to God, which is your spiritual worship.* (Romans 12:1)

[5] *Do not be conformed to this world, but be transformed by the renewing of your minds, so that you may discern what is the will of God—what is good and acceptable and perfect.* (Romans 12:2)

[6] *To open their eyes so that they may turn from darkness to light and from the power of Satan to God, so that they may receive forgiveness of sins and a place among those who are sanctified by faith in me.* (Acts 26:18)

[7] *Pursue peace with everyone, and the holiness without which no one will see the Lord.* (Hebrews 12:14)

[8] *For it is from within, from the human heart, that evil intentions come: fornication, theft, murder, adultery, avarice, wickedness, deceit, licentiousness, envy, slander, pride, folly.* (Mark 7:21–22)

[9] *Enter through the narrow gate; for the gate is wide and the road is easy that leads to destruction, and there are many who take it.* (Matthew 7:13)

[10] *But the cowardly, unbelieving, abominable, murderers, sexually immoral, sorcerers, idolaters, and all liars shall have their part in the lake which burns with fire and brimstone, which is the second death.* (Revelation 21:8 NKJV)

[11] Juvenal, Roman poet, ca. 55-127 CE.

[12] *Hope deferred makes the heart sick, but a desire fulfilled is a tree of life.* (Proverbs 13:12)

[13] *For the love of money is a root of all kinds of evil, for which some have strayed from the faith in their greediness, and pierced themselves through with many sorrows.* (1 Timothy 6:10 NKJV)

4

Myths About the New Birth

As I said in the beginning, here are a few inferences which naturally follow from the preceding observations.

Myth 1: The new birth is the same as baptism

First, it follows that baptism is not the new birth; they are not one and the same thing. Many people seem to think they are just the same — at least, they speak as if they thought so — but I do not know of any Christian denomination that teaches this.

For instance, the Calvinist position[1] is clearly declared in the *Larger Catechism:*[2]

Question: What are the parts of a sacrament? Answer: The parts of a sacrament are two, an outward physical sign, and an inward and spiritual grace the sign represents.

Question: What is baptism? Answer: Baptism is a

sacrament in which Christ commanded washing with water as a sign and seal of new birth by his Spirit.

Clearly baptism, the sign, is spoken of as distinct from new birth, the thing represented by the sign.

In the same way, the Church of England catechism declares its belief with the utmost clarity:

Question: What do you mean by this word, sacrament? Answer: I mean an outward and visible sign of an inward and spiritual grace.

Question: What is the outward part or form in baptism? Answer: Water, in which the person is baptized in the name of the Father, Son, and Holy Spirit.

Question: What is the inward part, or thing represented? Answer: A death to sin, and a new birth to righteousness.

Nothing, therefore, is plainer than the fact that, according to the Church of England, baptism is not the new birth.

But actually, the logic is so clear and evident that we do not need to quote any other authority. For what can be more plain than the fact that baptism is a visible thing, and the new birth is invisible, and therefore they are completely different from each other? One is the act of a person, washing the body. The other is a change worked by God in the soul. So baptism is just as different from the new birth as the soul is from the body, or water from the Holy Spirit.

Myth 2: Baptism and new birth always go together

All this leads us to our second observation: Just as the new birth is not the same thing as baptism, so it does not always accompany baptism: They do not constantly go together. A person may possibly be born of water and yet not be born of the Spirit.[3] There may sometimes be the outward sign, where there is not the inward grace.

I do not now speak with regard to infants. Our church certainly supposes that all who are baptized in their infancy are at the same time born again; the whole liturgy for the baptism of infants is based on this supposition.[4] And the fact that we don't understand how God can work this in an infant is not a major objection, because we don't really understand how God works it in a person of riper years, either.

But whatever the case with infants, it is certain that not every older person who is baptized is born again at the same time. The tree is known by its fruit.[5] So it appears too plain to be denied that some who were children of the devil before they were baptized continue the same after baptism, because they do the works of their father.[6] They continue as servants of sin, without even pretending to inward or outward holiness.

Myth 3: The new birth is the same as becoming holy

A third conclusion we may draw from what has been observed is that the new birth is not the same as sanctification, or becoming holy. Indeed, many take for granted that they are the same, particularly an eminent writer, in his late treatise on *The Nature and Grounds of Christian Regeneration*.[7]

Without considering several other weighty objections that might be made to that book, this is a key one: It all along speaks of the new birth as a progressive work, carried on in the soul by slow degrees, from the time of our first turning to God. This is undeniably true of sanctification, the process of being made holy; but of regeneration, the new birth, it is not true.

New birth is a part of sanctification, but not the whole thing; it is the gate to it, the entrance into it. When we are born again, then our sanctification, our inward and outward holiness, begins. From that point we are gradually to grow up in him who is our head.[8] This expression of the apostle Paul admirably illustrates the difference between one and the other, and further points out the exact parallel there is between natural and spiritual things.

A child is born of a woman in a moment, or at least in a very short time. Afterward she gradually and slowly grows until she reaches the size of an adult. In the same way, a child is born of God in a short time, if not in a moment. But it is by slow degrees that she afterward grows up to the measure of the full stature of Christ.

The same relation, therefore, which there is between our natural birth and our growth, there is also between our new birth and our sanctification.

Discussion Questions

1. Why might people think baptism and the new birth are the same thing?

2. Why might people think the new birth always accompanies baptism?

3. Under "Myth 2," Wesley implies that you can tell if a person has been born again by watching what they do. In the last chapter he said that good, honest, moral, church-going people who never hurt anyone still need to be born again.

Do you think Wesley would contradict himself on such an important point without realizing it?

How do you reconcile these two statements?

4. In the third section of this chapter Wesley publicly disagrees with a popular book written by a fellow Christian theologian.

When is such a public expression appropriate and when is it not?

What can we learn from the way in which Wesley expresses his disagreement?

5. "When we are born again, then our sanctification, our inward and outward holiness, begins. From that point we are gradually to 'grow up in him who is our head.'"

What are the signs of growing in inward and outward holiness?

How well are you progressing in your own personal spiritual growth?

What one or two things might you do to help this process?

Notes

[1] Calvinism is a theological orientation usually associated with Presbyterians, Congregationalists, and many Baptists. Most English Christians who were not Anglican or Roman Catholic held to some form of Calvinist theology. Wesley's point in quoting the Calvinist teaching is that even Christians who differ in many particulars agree that baptism is not new birth.

[2] *Westminster Larger Catechism*, Questions 163 and 165.

[3] *Jesus answered, "Very truly, I tell you, no one can enter the kingdom*

of God without being born of water and Spirit." (John 3:5)

[4] Wesley is not saying that anyone baptized as an infant will automatically go to heaven no matter what they do later in life. His point is to give comfort to the many parents in his day who had a child die in infancy.

[5] *Either make the tree good, and its fruit good; or make the tree bad, and its fruit bad; for the tree is known by its fruit.* (Matthew 12:33)

[6] *You are from your father the devil, and you choose to do your father's desires. He was a murderer from the beginning and does not stand in the truth, because there is no truth in him. When he lies, he speaks according to his own nature, for he is a liar and the father of lies.* (John 8:44)

[7] *The Grounds and Reasons of Christian Regeneration, or, The New-Birth, Offered to the Consideration of Christians and Deists,* by William Law, 1739.

[8] *But speaking the truth in love, we must grow up in every way into him who is the head, into Christ.* (Ephesians 4:15)

5

A Warning to the Spiritually Unborn

One point more we may learn from the preceding observations. But it is a point of such great importance that we must consider it very carefully and in some detail.

What should you say to a sinner?

What should someone who loves people, and is grieved at the thought of anyone perishing,[1] say to a person they see living a life of sabbath-breaking, drunkenness, or any other willful sin? What can they say, if all we've been talking about is true, but, "You must be born again?"[2]

"Wait," says a well-meaning person, "that can't be right. How can you talk so unkindly to them? Haven't they been baptized already? They can't be born again now."

They can't be born again? Is this your position? Then they cannot be saved. Though they be as old as Nicodemus was, Jesus said that unless they are born again, they cannot enter the kingdom of God.[3] So if you say they cannot be born again, you in effect condemn them to damnation.

Where lies the unkindness now? On my side, or on yours? I say they may be born again, and so become an heir of salvation. You say they cannot be born again. If that is true, they must inevitably perish! So you utterly block up their way to salvation, and send them to hell, because you want to be kind!

What do you say to those who trust in baptism for their salvation?

But perhaps it's the sinner himself, to whom in genuine kindness we say, "You must be born again," who has been taught to say, "I defy your new doctrine. I don't need to be born again. I was born again when I was baptized. What! Would you have me deny my baptism?"

There is nothing under heaven that can excuse a lie. Otherwise, my first answer to an open sinner would be, "If you have been baptized, don't admit it. Because that only makes you more guilty! That will only increase your damnation!"

Were you devoted to God at eight days old, and all these years you've been devoting yourself to the devil? Were you, even before you could think, given to God the Father, the Son, and the Holy Spirit, and now, ever since you can think for yourself, you've been flying in the face of God, and giving yourself to Satan? Does the abomination of desolation[4] — the love of the world, pride, anger, lust, foolish desire, and a whole train of vile affections — stand where it ought not? Have you set up all those cursed things in that soul which was once a temple of the

Holy Spirit,[5] set apart for a dwelling place of God in the Spirit,[6] solemnly given up to him? And do you glory in the fact that you once belonged to God? Oh, be ashamed! Blush! Hide yourself in the earth! Never boast again of what ought to fill you with consternation and make you ashamed before God and man!

My second answer is: You have already denied your baptism, in a most effective way. You have denied it a thousand and a thousand times; and you do so still, day by day. For in your baptism you renounced the devil and all his works. Whenever, therefore, you give place to him again, whenever you do any of the works of the devil, then you deny your baptism. You deny it by every willful sin; by every act of uncleanness, drunkenness, or revenge; by every obscene or profane word; by every oath that comes out of your mouth. Every time you profane the day of the Lord, you thereby deny your baptism. Indeed, you deny it every time you do anything to someone else that you would not want them to do to you.

My third answer is: Whether you are baptized or unbaptized, you must be born again. Otherwise it is impossible to be inwardly holy. And without both inward and outward holiness, you cannot be happy, even in this world, much less in the world to come.

What do you say to those who trust in their good works?

Perhaps you say, "Wait! I do no harm to anyone. I'm honest and fair in all my dealings. I don't curse or take the Lord's name in vain. I don't profane the Lord's day. I'm not a drunkard. I don't slander my neighbor. In fact, I don't live in any willful sin."

If this is true, I certainly wish that everyone went as far as you do. But you must go farther yet, or you cannot be saved: still, *you must be born again.*

Maybe you add, "I do go farther yet. I not only do no harm, but I do all the good I can?"

I doubt that fact; I suspect you have had a thousand opportunities of doing good which you have allowed to pass you by, and for which therefore you are accountable to God. But even if you had grasped every opportunity, even if you really had done all the good you possibly could to every person, even this doesn't change anything: still, *you must be born again.* Without that, none of the rest will do any good to your poor, sinful, polluted soul.

"But wait! I constantly practice all the spiritual disciples. I go to church and take Holy Communion."

Good for you! But all that will not keep you out of hell unless you are born again. Go to church twice a day; take Communion every week; say ever so many prayers in private; hear ever so many good sermons; read ever so many good books; still, *you must be born again*. None of these things will substitute for the new birth, and neither will anything else under heaven.

A prayer for the new birth

If you have not already experienced this inward work of God, let this be your continual prayer:

> *Lord, add this to all your blessings — let me be born again! Deny whatever you want, but don't deny this. Let me be born from above![]7 Take away whatever seems good to you — my reputation, money, friends, health — only give me this, to be born of the Spirit,[]8 to be counted among the children of God![]9 Let me be born, not of perishable seed, but imperishable,[]10 by the word of God, which lives and lasts forever![]11 And then let me daily grow in grace, and in the knowledge of our Lord and Savior Jesus Christ![]12*

Discussion Questions

1. If Wesley was preaching this sermon today, what habits or activities might he name as indicators of willful sin?

2. Have you ever hesitated to confront a person who was engaging in something you know the Bible condemns?
   Why?

3. Is it more kind to allow someone to continue in a path that leads them away from God, or to try to turn them toward God even if it means an uncomfortable conversation?

4. Have you ever thought of sin as denying your baptism? Does that idea change your perspective in any way?

5. Do you know anyone who believes they will go to heaven because they have lived a better life than other people?
   After going through this study, if they asked what you thought of that, what would you say to them?

6. Do you know anyone who believes they can never go to heaven because of some bad thing they have done?
   After going through this study, what would you say to them?

7. Are you familiar with what is commonly known as "The Sinner's Prayer?" Here is the Billy Graham version:

Dear Lord Jesus, I know that I am a sinner, and I ask for Your forgiveness. I believe You died for my sins and rose from the dead. I turn from my sins and invite You to come into my heart and life. I want to trust and follow You as my Lord and Savior. In Your Name. Amen.

How is the prayer at the end of Wesley's sermon different from that prayer?

How is it the same?

8. What have you gained from this study?

Would you be interested in doing another study in this series?

9. How would everyone feel about praying the Wesley's prayer for the new birth together right now?

Special Request

If you've enjoyed this study, please help others find it by posting a review. Thank you!

Notes

[1] *The Lord is not slow about his promise, as some think of slowness, but is patient with you, not wanting any to perish, but all to come to repentance.* (2 Peter 3:9)

[2] *Do not marvel that I said to you, "You must be born again."* (John 3:7 NKJV)

[3] *Jesus answered, "Very truly, I tell you, no one can enter the kingdom of God without being born of water and Spirit."* (John 3:5)

[4] *And forces shall be mustered by him, and they shall defile the sanctuary fortress; then they shall take away the daily sacrifices, and place there the abomination of desolation.* (Daniel 11:31 NKJV)

[5] *Do you not know that you are God's temple and that God's Spirit dwells in you?* (1 Corinthians 3:16)

[6] *in whom you also are built together spiritually into a dwelling place for God.* (Ephesians 2:22)

[7] *Born from above* is an alternate reading for John 3:7. The Greek word is *anothen.* It can refer to place, "from above;" or to time, "from the beginning," often in the sense of "start over again."

[8] *Jesus answered, "Very truly, I tell you, no one can enter the kingdom of God without being born of water and Spirit. What is born of the flesh is flesh, and what is born of the Spirit is spirit."* (John 3:5–6)

[9] *But to all who received him, who believed in his name, he gave power to become children of God.* (John 1:12)

[10] *So it is with the resurrection of the dead. What is sown is perishable, what is raised is imperishable.* (1 Corinthians 15:42)

[11] *The grass withers, the flower fades; but the word of our God will stand forever.* (Isaiah 40:8)

[12] *But grow in the grace and knowledge of our Lord and Savior Jesus Christ. To him be the glory both now and to the day of eternity. Amen.* (2 Peter 3:18)

Appendix: John Wesley's Original Words

The New Birth

by John Wesley

Sermon #45, from the Thomas Jackson edition of *The Works of John Wesley*, 1872. Enhanced version, from The Christian Classics Ethereal Library.

> *"Ye must be born again."* — John 3:7

1. If any doctrines within the whole compass of Christianity may be properly termed fundamental, they are doubtless these two, — the doctrine of justification, and that of the new birth: The former relating to that great work which God does for us, in forgiving our sins; the latter, to the great work which God does in us, in renewing our fallen nature. In order of time, neither of these is before the other: in the moment we are justified by the grace of God, through the redemption that is in Jesus, we are also "born of the Spirit;" but in order of thinking, as it is termed, justification precedes the new birth. We first conceive

his wrath to be turned away, and then his Spirit to work in our hearts.

2. How great importance then must it be of, to every child of man, thoroughly to understand these fundamental doctrines! From a full conviction of this, many excellent men have wrote very largely concerning justification, explaining every point relating thereto, and opening the Scriptures which treat upon it. Many likewise have wrote on the new birth: And some of them largely enough; but yet not so clearly as might have been desired, nor so deeply and accurately; having either given a dark, abstruse account of it, or a slight and superficial one. Therefore a full, and at the same time a clear, account of the new birth, seems to be wanting still; such as may enable us to give a satisfactory answer to these three questions: First, Why must we be born again? What is the foundation of this doctrine of the new birth? Secondly, How must we be born again? What is the nature of the new birth? And, Thirdly, Wherefore must we be born again? To what end is it necessary? These questions, by the assistance of God, I shall briefly and plainly answer; and then subjoin a few inferences which will naturally follow.

I. 1. And, First, Why must we be born again? What is the foundation of this doctrine? The foundation of it lies near as deep as the creation of the world; in the scriptural account whereof we read, "And God," the three-one God, "said, Let us make man in our image, after our likeness. So God created man in his own image, in the image of God created he him:" (Gen. 1:26, 27:) — Not barely in his natural image, a picture of his own immortality; a spiritual being, endued with understanding, freedom of will, and various affections; — nor merely in his political image, the governor of this lower world, having "dominion over the fishes of the sea, and over all the earth;" — but chiefly in his moral image; which, according to the Apostle, is "righteousness and true holiness." (Eph. 4:24.) In this image of God was man made. "God is love:" Accordingly, man at his creation was full of love; which was the sole principle of all his tempers, thoughts, words, and actions. God is full of justice, mercy, and truth; so was man as he came from the hands of his Creator. God is spotless purity; and so man was in the beginning pure from every sinful blot; otherwise God could not have pronounced him, as well as all the other work of his hands, "very good" (Gen. 1:31.) This he could not have been, had he not been pure from sin, and filled with righteousness and true holiness. For there is no medium: If we suppose an intelligent creature not to love God, not to be righteous and holy, we necessarily suppose him not to be good at all; much less to be "very good."

2. But, although man was made in the image of God, yet he was not made immutable. This would have been inconsistent with the state of trial in which God was pleased to place him. He was therefore created able to stand, and yet liable to fall. And this God himself apprized him of, and gave him a solemn warning against it. Nevertheless, man did not abide in honour: He fell from his high estate. He "ate of the tree whereof the Lord had commanded him, Thou shalt not eat thereof." By this willful act of disobedience to his Creator, this flat rebellion against his Sovereign, he openly declared that he would no longer have God to rule over him; That he would be governed by his own will, and not the will of Him that created him; and that he would not seek his happiness in God, but in the world, in the works of his hands. Now, God had told him before, "In the day that thou eatest" of that fruit, "thou shalt surely die." And the word of

the Lord cannot be broken. Accordingly, in that day he did die: He died to God, — the most dreadful of all deaths. He lost the life of God: He was separated from Him, in union with whom his spiritual life consisted. The body dies when it is separated from the soul; the soul, when it is separated from God. But this separation from God, Adam sustained in the day, the hour, he ate of the forbidden fruit. And of this he gave immediate proof; presently showing by his behaviour, that the love of God was extinguished in his soul, which was now "alienated from the life of God." Instead of this, he was now under the power of servile fear, so that he fled from the presence of the Lord. Yea, so little did he retain even of the knowledge of Him who filleth heaven and earth, that he endeavored to "hide himself from the Lord God among the trees of the garden:" (Gen. 3:8:) So had he lost both the knowledge and the love of God, without which the image of God could not subsist. Of this, therefore, he was deprived at the same time, and became unholy as well as unhappy. In the room of this, he had sunk into pride and self-will, the very image of the devil; and into sensual appetites and desires, the image of the beasts that perish.

3. If it be said, "Nay, but that threatening, 'In the day that thou eatest thereof, thou shalt surely die,' refers to temporal death, and that alone, to the death of the body only;" the answer is plain: To affirm this is flatly and palpably to make God a liar; to aver that the God of truth positively affirmed a thing contrary to truth. For it is evident, Adam did not die in this sense, "in the day that he ate thereof." He lived, in the sense opposite to this death, above nine hundred years after. So that this cannot possibly be understood of the death of the body, without impeaching the veracity of God. It must therefore be understood of spiritual death, the loss of the life and image of

48

God.

4. And in Adam all died, all human kind, all the children of men who were then in Adam's loins. The natural consequence of this is, that every one descended from him comes into the world spiritually dead, dead to God, wholly dead in sin; entirely void of the life of God; void of the image of God, of all that righteousness and holiness wherein Adam was created. Instead of this, every man born into the world now bears the image of the devil in pride and self-will; the image of the beast, in sensual appetites and desires. This, then, is the foundation of the new birth, — the entire corruption of our nature. Hence it is, that, being born in sin, we must be "born again." Hence every one that is born of a woman must be born of the Spirit of God.

II. 1. But how must a man be born again? What is the nature of the new birth? This is the Second question. And a question it is of the highest moment that can be conceived. We ought not, therefore, in so weighty a concern, to be content with a slight inquiry; but to examine it with all possible care, and to ponder it in our hearts, till we fully understand this important point, and clearly see how we are to be born again.

2. Not that we are to expect any minute, philosophical account of the manner how this is done. Our Lord sufficiently guards us against any such expectation, by the words immediately following the text; wherein he reminds Nicodemus of as indisputable a fact as any in the whole compass of nature, which, notwithstanding, the wisest man under the sun is not able fully to explain. "The wind bloweth where it listeth," — not by thy power or wisdom; "and thou hearest the sound thereof;" — thou art absolutely assured, beyond all doubt, that it doth blow; "but thou canst not tell whence it cometh, nor whither

it goeth;" — the precise manner how it begins and ends, rises and falls, no man can tell. "So is every one that is born of the Spirit:" — Thou mayest be as absolutely assured of the fact, as of the blowing of the wind; but the precise manner how it is done, how the Holy Spirit works this in the soul, neither thou nor the wisest of the children of men is able to explain.

3. However, it suffices for every rational and Christian purpose, that, without descending into curious, critical inquiries, we can give a plain scriptural account of the nature of the new birth. This will satisfy every reasonable man, who desires only the salvation of his soul. The expression, "being born again," was not first used by our Lord in his conversation with Nicodemus: It was well known before that time, and was in common use among the Jews when our Saviour appeared among them. When an adult Heathen was convinced that the Jewish religion was of God, and desired to join therein, it was the custom to baptize him first, before he was admitted to circumcision. And when he was baptized, he was said to be born again; by which they meant, that he who was before a child of the devil was now adopted into the family of God, and accounted one of his children. This expression, therefore, which Nicodemus, being "a Teacher in Israel," ought to have understood well, our Lord uses in conversing with him; only in a stronger sense than he was accustomed to. And this might be the reason of his asking, "How can these things be?" They cannot be literally: — A man cannot "enter a second time into his mother's womb, and be born:" — But they may spiritually: A man may be born from above, born of God, born of the Spirit, in a manner which bears a very near analogy to the natural birth.

4. Before a child is born into the world he has eyes, but sees not; he has ears, but does not hear. He has a very imperfect use

of any other sense. He has no knowledge of any of the things of the world, or any natural understanding. To that manner of existence which he then has, we do not even give the name of life. It is then only when a man is born, that we say he begins to live. For as soon as he is born, be begins to see the light, and the various objects with which he is encompassed. His ears are then opened, and he hears the sounds which successively strike upon them. At the same time, all the other organs of sense begin to be exercised upon their proper objects. He likewise breathes, and lives in a manner wholly different from what he did before. How exactly doth the parallel hold in all these instances! While a man is in a mere natural state, before he is born of God, he has, in a spiritual sense, eyes and sees not; a thick impenetrable veil lies upon them; he has ears, but hears not; he is utterly deaf to what he is most of all concerned to hear. His other spiritual senses are all locked up: He is in the same condition as if he had them not. Hence he has no knowledge of God; no intercourse with him; he is not at all acquainted with him. He has no true knowledge of the things of God, either of spiritual or eternal things; therefore, though he is a living man, he is a dead Christian. But as soon as he is born of God, there is a total change in all these particulars. The "eyes of his understanding are opened;" (such is the language of the great Apostle;) and, He who of old "commanded light to shine out of darkness shining on his heart, he sees the light of the glory of God," his glorious love, "in the face of Jesus Christ." His ears being opened, he is now capable of hearing the inward voice of God, saying, "Be of good cheer; thy sins are forgiven thee;" "go and sin no more." This is the purport of what God speaks to his heart; although perhaps not in these very words. He is now ready to hear whatsoever "He that teacheth man knowledge" is pleased, from time to time, to reveal to him. He "feels in his heart," to use the language of our Church, "the mighty working of the Spirit of God;" not in a gross, carnal sense as the men of the world stupidly and willfully misunderstand the expression; though they have been told again and again, we mean thereby neither more nor less than this: He feels, is inwardly sensible of, the graces which the Spirit of God works in his heart. He feels, he is conscious of, a "peace which passeth all understanding." He many times feels such a joy in God as is "unspeakable, and full of glory." He feels "the love of God shed abroad in his heart by the Holy Ghost which is given unto him;" and all his spiritual senses are then exercised to discern spiritual good and evil. By the use of these, he is daily increasing in the knowledge of God, of Jesus Christ whom he hath sent and to all the things pertaining to his inward kingdom. And now he may be properly said to live: God having quickened him by his Spirit, he is alive to God through Jesus Christ. He lives a life which the world knoweth not of, a "life which is hid with Christ in God." God is continually breathing, as it were, upon the soul; and his soul is breathing unto God. Grace is descending into his heart; and prayer and praise ascending to heaven: And by this intercourse between God and man, this fellowship with the Father and the Son, as by a kind of spiritual respiration, the life of God in the soul is sustained; and the child of God grows up, till he comes to the "full measure of the stature of Christ."

5. From hence it manifestly appears, what is the nature of the new birth. It is that great change which God works in the soul when he brings it into life; when he raises it from the death of sin to the life of righteousness. It is the change wrought in the whole soul by the almighty Spirit of God when it is "created anew in Christ Jesus;" when it is "renewed after the image of

God, in righteousness and true holiness;" when the love of the world is changed into the love of God; pride into humility; passion into meekness; hatred, envy, malice, into a sincere, tender, disinterested love for all mankind. In a word, it is that change whereby the earthly, sensual, devilish mind is turned into the "mind which was in Christ Jesus." This is the nature of the new birth: "So is every one that is born of the Spirit."

III. 1. It is not difficult for any who has considered these things, to see the necessity of the new birth, and to answer the Third question, Wherefore, to what end, is it necessary that we should be born again? It is very easily discerned, that this is necessary, First, in order to holiness. For what is holiness according to the oracles of God? Not a bare external religion, a round of outward duties, how many soever they be, and how exactly soever performed. No: Gospel holiness is no less than the image of God stamped upon the heart; it is no other than the whole mind which was in Christ Jesus; it consists of all heavenly affections and tempers mingled together in one. It implies such a continual, thankful love to Him who hath not withheld from us his Son, his only son, as makes it natural, and in a manner necessary to us, to love every child of man; as fills us "with bowels of mercies, kindness, gentleness, long-suffering:" It is such a love of God as teaches us to be blameless in all manner of conversation; as enables us to present our souls and bodies, all we are and all we have, all our thoughts, words, and actions, a continual sacrifice to God, acceptable through Christ Jesus. Now, this holiness can have no existence till we are renewed in the image of our mind. It cannot commence in the soul till that change be wrought; till, by the power of the Highest overshadowing us, we are "brought from darkness to light, from the power of Satan unto God;" that is, till we are born again; which, therefore, is absolutely necessary in order to holiness.

2. But "without holiness no man shall see the Lord," shall see the face of God in glory. Of consequence, the new birth is absolutely necessary in order to eternal salvation. Men may indeed flatter themselves (so desperately wicked and so deceitful is the heart of man!) that they may live in their sins till they come to the last gasp, and yet afterwards live with God; and thousands do really believe, that they have found a broad way which leadeth not to destruction. "What danger," say they, "can a woman be in that is so harmless and so virtuous? What fear is there that so honest a man, one of so strict morality, should miss of heaven; especially if, over and above all this, they constantly attend on church and sacrament?" One of these will ask with all assurance, "What! Shall not I do as well as my neighbours?" Yes as well as your unholy neighbours; as well as your neighbours that die in their sins! For you will all drop into the pit together, into the nethermost hell! You will all lie together in the lake of fire; "the lake of fire burning with brimstone." Then, at length, you will see (but God grant you may see it before!) the necessity of holiness in order to glory; and, consequently, of the new birth, since none can be holy, except he be born again.

3. For the same reason, except he be born again, none can be happy even in this world. For it is not possible, in the nature of things, that a man should be happy who is not holy. Even the poor, ungodly poet could tell us, Nemo malus felix: "no wicked man is happy." The reason is plain: All unholy tempers are uneasy tempers: Not only malice, hatred, envy jealousy, revenge, create a present hell in the breast; but even the softer passions, if not kept within due bounds, give a thousand times

more pain than pleasure. Even "hope," when "deferred," (and how often must this be the case!) "maketh the heart sick;" and every desire which is not according to the will of God is liable to "pierce" us "through with many sorrows:" And all those general sources of sin — pride, self-will, and idolatry — are, in the same proportion as they prevail, general sources of misery. Therefore, as long as these reign in any soul, happiness has no place there. But they must reign till the bent of our nature is changed, that is, till we are born again; consequently, the new birth is absolutely necessary in order to happiness in this world, as well as in the world to come.

IV. I proposed in the Last place to subjoin a few inferences, which naturally follow from the preceding observations.

1. And, First, it follows, that baptism is not the new birth: They are not one and the same thing. Many indeed seem to imagine that they are just the same; at least, they speak as if they thought so; but I do not know that this opinion is publicly avowed by any denomination of Christians whatever. Certainly it is not by any within these kingdoms, whether of the established Church, or dissenting from it. The judgment of the latter is clearly declared in the large Catechism. [Q. 163, 165. — Ed.] — Q. "What are the parts of a sacrament? A. The parts of a sacrament are two: The one an outward outward and sensible sign; the other, and inward and spiritual grace, thereby signified. — Q. What is baptism? A. Baptism is a sacrament, wherein Christ hath ordained the washing with water, to be a sign and seal of regeneration by his Spirit." Here it is manifest, baptism, the sign, is spoken of as distinct from regeneration, the thing signified. In the Church Catechism likewise, the judgment of our Church is declared with the utmost clearness: "What

meanest thou by this word, sacrament? A. I mean an outward and visible sign of an inward and spiritual grace. Q. What is the outward part or form in baptism? A. Water, wherein the person is baptized, in the name of the Father, Son, and Holy Ghost. Q. What is the inward part, or thing signified? A. A death unto sin, and a new birth unto righteousness." Nothing, therefore, is plainer than that, according to the Church of England, baptism is not the new birth. But indeed the reason of the thing is so clear and evident, as not to need any other authority. For what can be more plain, than the one is a visible, the other an invisible thing, and therefore wholly different from each other? — the one being an act of man, purifying the body; the other a change wrought by God in the soul: So that the former is just as distinguishable from the latter, as the soul from the body, or water from the Holy Ghost.

2. From the preceding reflections we may, Secondly, observe, that as the new birth is not the same thing with baptism, so it does not always accompany baptism: They do not constantly go together. A man my possibly be "born of water," and yet not be "born of the Spirit." There may sometimes be the outward sign, where there is not the inward grace. I do not now speak with regard to infants: It is certain our Church supposes that all who are baptized in their infancy are at the same time born again; and it is allowed that the whole Office for the Baptism of Infants proceeds upon this supposition. Nor is it an objection of any weight against this, that we cannot comprehend how this work can be wrought in infants. For neither can we comprehend how it is wrought in a person of riper years. But whatever be the case with infants, it is sure all of riper years who are baptized are not at the same time born again. "The tree is known by its fruits:" And hereby it appears too plain to be denied, that

divers of those who were children of the devil before they were baptized continue the same after baptism: "for the works of their father they do:" They continue servants of sin, without any pretense either to inward or outward holiness.

3. A Third inference which we may draw from what has been observed, is, that the new birth is not the same with sanctification. This is indeed taken for granted by many; particularly by an eminent writer, in his late treatise on "The Nature and Grounds of Christian Regeneration." To waive several other weighty objections which might be made to that tract, this is a palpable one: It all along speaks of regeneration as a progressive work, carried on in the soul by slow degrees, from the time of our first turning to God. This is undeniably true of sanctification; but of regeneration, the new birth, it is not true. This is a part of sanctification, not the whole; it is the gate to it, the entrance into it. When we are born again, then our sanctification, our inward and outward holiness, begins; and thenceforward we are gradually to "grow up in Him who is our Head." This expression of the Apostle admirably illustrates the difference between one and the other, and farther points out the exact analogy there is between natural and spiritual things. A child is born of a woman in a moment, or at least in a very short time: Afterward he gradually and slowly grows, till he attains to the stature of a man. In like manner, a child is born of God in a short time, if not in a moment. But it is by slow degrees that he afterward grows up to the measure of the full stature of Christ. The same relation, therefore, which there is between our natural birth and our growth, there is also between our new birth and our sanctification.

4. One point more we may learn from the preceding observations. But it is a point of so great importance, as may

excuse the considering it the more carefully, and prosecuting it at some length. What must one who loves the souls of men, and is grieved that any of them should perish, say to one whom he sees living in sabbath-breaking, drunkenness, or any other willful sin? What can he say, if the foregoing observations are true, but, "You must be born again?" "No," says a zealous man, "that cannot be. How can you talk so uncharitably to the man? Has he not been baptized already? He cannot be born again now." Can he not be born again? Do you affirm this? Then he cannot be saved. Though he be as old as Nicodemus was, yet "except he be born again, he cannot see the kingdom of God." Therefore in saying, "He cannot be born again," you in effect deliver him over to damnation. And where lies the uncharitableness now? — on my side, or on yours? I say, he may be born again, and so become an heir of salvation. You say, "He cannot be born again:" And if so, he must inevitably perish! So you utterly block up his way to salvation, and send him to hell, out of mere charity! But perhaps the sinner himself, to whom in real charity we say, "You must be born again," has been taught to say, "I defy your new doctrine; I need not be born again: I was born again when I was baptized. What! Would you have me deny my baptism?" I answer, First, There is nothing under heaven which can excuse a lie; otherwise I should say to an open sinner, If you have been baptized, do not own it. For how highly does this aggravate your guilt! How will it increase your damnation! Was you devoted to God at eight days old, and have you been all these years devoting yourself to the devil? Was you, even before you had the use of reason, consecrated to God the Father, the Son, and the Holy Ghost? And have you, ever since you had the use of it, been flying in the face of God, and consecrating yourself to Satan? Does the abomination of desolation — the love of the world, pride, anger, lust, foolish desire, and a whole train of vile affections — stand where it ought not? Have you set up all the accursed things in that soul which was once a temple of the Holy Ghost; set apart for an "habitation of God, through the Spirit;" yea, solemnly given up to him? And do you glory in this, that you once belonged to God? Oh be ashamed ! blush ! hide yourself in the earth ! Never boast more of what ought to fill you with confusion, to make you ashamed before God and man! I answer, Secondly, You have already denied your baptism; and that in the most effectual manner. You have denied it a thousand and a thousand times; and you do so still, day by day. For in your baptism you renounced the devil and all his works. Whenever, therefore, you give place to him again, whenever you do any of the works of the devil, then you deny your baptism. Therefore you deny it by every willful sin; by every act of uncleanness, drunkenness, or revenge; by every obscene or profane word; by every oath that comes out of your mouth. Every time you profane the day of the Lord, you thereby deny your baptism; yea, every time you do any thing to another which you would not he should do to you. I answer, Thirdly, Be you baptized or unbaptized, "you must be born again;" otherwise it is not possible you should be inwardly holy; and without inward as well as outward holiness, you cannot be happy, even in this world, much less in the world to come. Do you say, "Nay, but I do no harm to any man; I am honest and just in all my dealings; I do not curse, or take the Lord's name in vain; I do not profane the Lord's day; I am no drunkard; I do not slander my neighbour, nor live in any willful sin?" If this be so, it were much to be wished that all men went as far as you do. But you must go farther yet, or you cannot be saved: Still, "you must be born again." Do you add, "I do go farther yet; for I not only do no harm, but do all the good I can?" I doubt that fact; I fear you have had a thousand opportunities of doing good which you have suffered to pass by unimproved, and for which therefore you are accountable to God. But if you had improved them all, if you really had done all the good you possibly could to all men, yet this does not at all alter the case; still, "you must be born again." Without this nothing will do any good to your poor, sinful, polluted soul. "Nay, but I constantly attend all the ordinances of God: I keep to my church and sacrament." It is well you do: But all this will not keep you from hell, except you be born again. Go to church twice a day; go to the Lord's table every week; say ever so many prayers in private; hear ever so many good sermons; read ever so many good books; still, "you must be born again:" None of these things will stand in the place of the new birth; no, nor any thing under heaven. Let this therefore, if you have not already experienced this inward work of God, be your continual prayer: "Lord, add this to all thy blessings, — let me be born again! Deny whatever thou pleasest, but deny not this; let me be 'born from above!' Take away whatsoever seemeth thee good, — reputation, fortune, friends, health, — only give me this, to be born of the Spirit, to be received among the children of God! Let me be born, 'not of corruptible seed, but incorruptible, by the word of God, which liveth and abideth for ever;' and then let me daily 'grow in grace, and in the knowledge of our Lord and Saviour Jesus Christ!'"

Notes

[1] Wesley, John. *Sermons on Several Occasions - Enhanced Version.* Thomas Jackson edition, 1872. Christian Classics Ethereal Library.

About the Author

Best known internationally as author of **Pastoring: The Nuts and Bolts**, in print in seven languages, David Wentz has a passion for helping people connect with God and make a difference. Combining 38 years as a pastor with a first career in engineering and graduate degrees from three very different seminaries (charismatic, mainstream, and Wesleyan-evangelical), he expresses God's truth in ways everyone can appreciate.

Raised in the Episcopal church, Dr. Wentz has also been part of Nazarene, Pentecostal Holiness, and non-denominational congregations. As a Methodist pastor he served small, large, and multicultural churches in rural, small-town, suburban, and urban settings, served as a regional church consultant in the Maryland – D.C. area, and led workshops for pastors internationally. In 2015 he retired to the rural Ozarks, where he writes, works in God's great outdoors, and oversees Doing Christianity, Inc., a small non-profit devoted to equipping pastors in developing and minority-Christian countries.

In 1974, David married his college sweetheart, Paula. They have five children and fourteen grandchildren.

The book of Ezekiel describes David's calling. Twenty-five

hundred years ago God called Ezekiel to teach God's ways and proclaim the Holy Spirit, the one who revives dry bones and forms them into a dwelling for God and a source of living water that heals nations.

Bones are still dry today. God still wants to dwell among his people. Nations still need healing. And people still need to be taught God's ways and be moved by God's Spirit. That's what David calls "Doing Christianity."

You can connect with me on:
🌐 https://www.pastordavidwentz.com
❖ https://www.facebook.com/profile.php?id=100064901162331

Subscribe to my newsletter:
✉   https://mailchi.mp/c162e27f817b/doing-christianity-email-newsletter-sign-up

Also by David Wentz

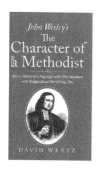

John Wesley's The Character of a Methodist: Set in Modern Language with Introduction and Suggestions for Group Use

"An excellent small group study." – Rev. Travis Knoll

In a time of upheaval in the largest denomination of the Methodist movement, this classic explanation and defense of Methodist Christianity by its founder is required reading. Pastor David Wentz has updated Wesley's 18th-century language, deleted references to no-longer-relevant theological disputes, and added an introduction that sets the work in context. The result is a clear, easy to read text that is enjoyable and understandable for modern readers of all levels of theological interest and expertise.

This short book is ideal for small groups and adult Sunday School classes as well as individual reading. Dr. Wentz has included thoughtful discussion questions at the end of each section, a brief guide on how to lead small groups, and a suggested six-week schedule. For further study, Wesley's numerous Scripture quotes and allusions are identified, with the Biblical text cited and quoted in footnotes. Wesley's full original version is included as an appendix.

No matter where one stands in the wide umbrella of worldwide Methodism, this accessible summary of its root emphases provides a vital foundation.

"I am planning to use my copy for a Confirmation class for adults and youth! I'll purchase some extra copies."

"So timely and so needed! Thank you for providing this valuable resource at a critical time for the Methodist Church."

Part of the John Wesley in Modern Language series

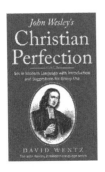

John Wesley's Christian Perfection: Set in Modern Language with Introduction and Suggestions for Group Use
"This book thrilled my soul and reinvigorated my hope." — Amazon reviewer

"Christians aren't perfect, just forgiven." **John Wesley doesn't agree.**

In this classic sermon, the father of Methodism and grandfather of the Salvation Army and the Pentecostal movement shows that under a proper Biblical definition, Christians not only can become perfect in this life — God commands us to!

Seeking perfection was an integral part of the explosive growth of Methodism for 100 years, even as it led to the persecution of those who practiced it. As many of the denominations descended from Wesley face turmoil and rebirth around the world, renewed attention to its theological roots is imperative.

Wesley pulls no punches in his closely-argued Biblical logic, but his 18th-century English is unfamiliar to modern readers. Long-time pastor David Wentz has updated the language to restore its original force and spirit. The result is a text that readers of all levels of theological interest and expertise will understand and enjoy.

Pastoring Revival: What to Do After the Holy Spirit Moves

"It's hard to put to words how excited this book makes me. I have pastored for years . . . Read this book, and get ready." — Amazon reviewer

"Come, Holy Spirit!" is a common prayer, but few pastors are trained what to do if God answers with unusual power.

Spiritual outbreaks at Asbury University and other places show that the cycle of American revivals is rolling around again. Only God can ignite revival, but he uses pastors to grow and guard it. Yet Bible colleges and seminaries rarely address revival outside of church history classes.

***Pastoring Revival: What to Do After the Holy Spirit Moves* will equip you to:**

- Understand how God has worked in past revivals
- Discern what is of God and what is of merely human origin, or worse
- Prepare for the unique decisions, problems, and opportunities of a church in revival
- Shepherd revival in a way that will strengthen rather than divide your church
- Grow your own spirit and maintain your health through it all

Drawing on two fascinating case studies, academic research, and his own thirty-eight years as a pastor, seeker, and student of revival, Dr. Wentz has produced a practical, engaging, Biblical, actionable guide to prepare every pastor for the next great move of God.

Don't wait to prepare for revival until after it hits!

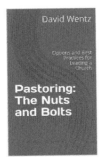

Pastoring: The Nuts and Bolts — Options and Best Practices for Leading a Church
Translated into seven languages and counting, Dr. Wentz's book has trained thousands of pastors around the world. It is the textbook for the 3-credit course MIN 315 offered by Christian Leaders Institute (along with the associated *Application Guide).* Seasoned pastors as well as those just starting praise its valuable insights.

Part One suggests three purposes of God the Father for his family, the church: becoming a spiritual dwelling (worship), raising God's children (discipleship), and inviting everyone into the family (evangelism).

Part Two draws on experience to illustrate advice on pastoral life, from call through personal and family issues to moving and retirement.

Part Three gives practical tips on leadership, preaching, worship, ministries, buildings, finances, administration, working with other churches, and dealing with problems.

A pastor for 38 years, Dr. Wentz holds advanced degrees from evangelical, mainline, and charismatic seminaries. He is the author of three other books.

If a pastor or church can have only one book besides the Bible, this is designed to be most helpful.

Pastoring: The Nuts and Bolts Application Guide

Pastors and Bible schools around the world hail *Pastoring: The Nuts and Bolts* as a comprehensive and accessible handbook of options and best practices for being a pastor and leading a church. Meant for pastors of every country and culture, every Christian theological leaning, and every denomination or none, it's a treasury of principles waiting to be applied.

That's where this **Application Guide** comes in. Full of thoughtful questions and exercises, it takes the general principles from **Pastoring** and makes them yours. Some questions will make you think and pray about what you believe and why. Others will take you from, "Hey, that's a good idea!" to "Here's an action plan for my church.

Every time your ministry changes, these exercises will give you a brand new strategy, customized by you for your specific situation, ready to implement.

NOTE: This is not a stand-alone book. This *Application Guide* requires the book, *Pastoring: The Nuts and Bolts — Options and Best Practices for Leading a Church.*

"Clear and powerful." "Stimulating." "Will make me understand myself better." "There is so much here." "I praise God for this application guide."

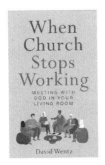

When Church Stops Working: Meeting With God in Your Living Room
If church has stopped working for you, but your spirit knows something is missing, God may be calling you to try something new.

Jesus promised, *"Where two or three gather together as my followers, I am there among them."* With a few friends and a little faith, anyone can claim that promise and experience the love and power that turned the world upside down.

David Wentz trains pastors around the world to equip God's people to be the church and have church any time, any place, with anybody. In this #1 bestseller, he walks you through meeting with God in your own living room with positive practical advice suited to every religious background or none.

It's how Christians gathered in the New Testament and the American frontier, and it's a growing movement around the world today.

(**Note to pastors:** this book is a proven way to extend your reach by mentoring living-room church leaders or developing living-room church networks.)

You don't need a seminary degree. You don't need a special building. All you need is a few friends and a little faith.

"What a refreshing read! Balanced in viewpoint and refraining from church-bashing, I found this book to be a practical guide and a breath of fresh air! A quality book that will make waves as we enter a time of church reformation in the coming years."